The Child's Acquisition of Language

The Child's Acquisition of Language

June Derrick

NFER Publishing Company Ltd.

Published by the NFER Publishing Company Ltd.,
2 Jennings Buildings, Thames Avenue,
Windsor, Berks. SL4 1QS
Registered Office: The Mere, Upton Park, Slough, Berks. SL1 2DQ
First published 1976
© National Foundation for Educational Research in England
and Wales, 1977
ISBN 0 85633 110 4

Typeset by Cameographics, 63 Milford Road, Reading RG1 8LG.
Printed in Great Britain by
Biddles of Guildford Martyr Road, Guildford, Surrey.
Distributed in the USA by Humanities Press Inc.,
Atlantic Highlands, New Jersey 07716 USA.

Contents

INTRODUCTION

Throughout this century and earlier people have been interested in how young children acquire their mother tongue. There are available to us from the 1890s onwards diary studies, i.e. records of the utterances made by infants from their first months of life. These, of course, were written records, with attempts to find a notation that actually gave an idea of the sounds, and combinations of sounds, produced by the young child. No doubt behind the keeping of these records was the same sense of wonder and pleasure that anyone has who watches the development of a child and hears his speech grow, listening for the first recognizable word, progressing to where the child begins to 'put words together', and thence to long stretches of connected words and syllables, rhymes and rituals and 'funny' sayings. Long before the child starts school he already seems to be able to say anything he wants to say. Within a couple of years he has developed from being *infans,* one without speech, to a person who uses the same complex language system as the adults around him with fluency and inventiveness.

Within this field of knowledge there comes an amazing spurt of activity in the last twelve years and a great outpouring of new studies, principally by linguists and psycholinguists. 'All over the world,' says Roger Brown, 'the first sentences of small children are being painstakingly taped, transcribed, and analysed as if they were the last sayings of great sages. Which is a surprising fate for the likes of: *That doggie, No more milk*, and *Hit ball'.* Indeed Roger Brown's own work on data such as those he cites is probably the fullest, and certainly the weightiest, analysis of children's early utterances and is drawn on extensively in what follows. Moreover, no one has described as lucidly as he the debt of all workers in this field to the grammatical theories of Noam Chomsky. In particular he points to Chomsky's *Syntactic Structures* (1957), a key work in all subsequent linguistic study, and Chomsky's thesis on the *generative* nature of grammar. A great deal that was thought and written about language until Chomsky's work appeared stressed not so much the rule-governed nature of language as the acquisition of language as a form of behaviour learnt by imitation, or by behavioural mechanisms (i.e. rewards reinforcing 'good' or acceptable behaviour). Chomsky pointed to the inadequacy of a view of language acquisition based on this thinking. Language is not a repertoire of sentences that is simply heard, imitated and learnt. Everyone, including the very young child, is constantly producing utterances that have not been made by anyone else. In acquiring language the child learns a rule system that makes it possible to produce a literally infinite variety of sentences. It is in this sense that Chomsky's term *generative* is used. The rules can generate an infinite number of sentences; in acquiring language we learn the rules, and thence the ability to generate the sentences we need for our purposes. The rules thus learnt are explicit neither for the child, nor, for the most part, the average adult, but in learning them one learns too to make and respond to grammatically acceptable, well-formed utterances, and to reject utterances that do not conform to the rules.

But what is the process by which the rules are learnt? What stages does the child go through before his speech approximates to that of the mature adult? Are these stages the same for all children? Are they the same for children learning different languages? And what are the forces that so condition this learning that by the age of 3½ or 4 young children seem to be able to use language in very different ways, with the result that, in contemporary educational jargon, some are linguistically advantaged, or favoured, and some disadvantaged or unfavoured? If we know something about the causes of these conditions, can we do anything about them, especially to help the unfavoured to match up to their more favoured peers? These are important questions for those concerned with the education of young children, and the report that follows discusses some of the answers. In the first chapter an account is given of the stages the young child goes through in acquiring his mother tongue. This is an attempt to synthesize the main lines of development traced in the literature, and to highlight the issues that seem to have the greatest relevance. In the second chapter the mother's role in this process is examined. This leads to an examination of what is in the mother's behaviour that fosters the child's language development, and to the notion that language is fostered differently in different homes. In the third chapter there is some discussion of two approaches to intervention in the child's language education, i.e. either through nursery (pre-school) education or in the home itself. The final chapter highlights some of the areas requiring research and development. In order to make the text more readable to the general 'lay' reader, references within it have been kept to the minimum. The major sources are listed in the Bibliography. A short annotated bibliography is provided in addition as a guide to those who wish to explore some of the literature for themselves. In it titles have been kept to the minimum. All of them are in print and should be easily available.

The compilation of this report was made possible by a grant received from the Department of Education and Science.

Chapter One

Language Development

Most adults acquire a very simple knowledge of human development. If they become parents they learn from their own observation of their children and also from the comments of grandparents, or friends, or health visitors. They begin to look out for changes in their baby's behaviour. From lying fairly still, unable to focus his eyes, and unable to raise his head, the baby begins to 'see' people, to exercise his arms and legs, to turn his head, eventually to be held with his head unsupported. He becomes responsive to people who peep into his cot, who pull faces at him, who lift him up, give him food, or make noises at him. At first he cries when in a state of discomfort. Later he begins to coo and chuckle, and to make a wide range of noises. There are, as it were, a series of milestones in a baby's life, and fair agreement about when the average baby reaches each one. They are part of the folklore of parenthood, and can be used to excite, to reassure or to worry the parents. The baby can be expected to smile at 6 weeks, to sit unsupported at 6 months, to stand or walk at 12 months, to say a small number of words between 12 and 18 months, and to 'put words together' at 18 months to 2 years.

Whatever the exceptions to the observed pattern of development, there is a sufficiently clear pattern in speech as in other skills, for it to be generally describable. It is also clearly identifiable as a feature of the maturation of the child. Children do not begin to put words together at a certain time because all mothers start training them to do so at that time. Nor do the child's needs suddenly change so that it becomes necessary for him to speak whereas before he did not. The only possible explanation for the onset of speech is that the child matures and speech then becomes possible, just as certain motor skills become possible at points in the child's development. Although language and motor development in young children can be traced in parallel sequences, the evidence suggests that these are parallel and not interdependent sequences. Although speech requires very precise control of tongue, lips and other speech organs, this control may already be acquired to a fine degree (for instance, in the child who can babble in long 'sentences', and say a large number of individual words intelligibly) without the child embarking on connected speech — however hard his parents try to train him to connect words together. He will only begin to do this later. The fact that very young children comprehend far more language than they are able to produce, also points to the separateness of language development from motor development. With this clear in our minds, then, it is interesting to look at the following tabulation of language and motor development. It summarizes what its author, Lenneberg, calls 'a gradual unfolding of capacities' and will serve here to outline the main features of speech described below.

The simultaneous development of language and coordination:

Age in Months	Vocalization and Language	Motor Development
4	Coos and chuckles.	Head self-supported; tonic neck reflex subsiding; can sit with pillow props on three sides.
6 to 9	Babbles; produces sounds such as 'ma' or 'da'; reduplication of sounds common.	Sits alone; pulls himself to standing; prompt unilateral reaching; first thumb opposition of grasp.
12 to 18	A small number of 'words'; follows simple commands and responds to 'no'.	Stands momentarily alone; creeps (i.e. crawls); walks sideways when holding on to a railing; takes a few steps when held by hands; grasp, prehension, and release fully developed.
18 to 21	From about 20 words at 18 months to about 200 words at 21; points to many more objects; comprehends simple questions; forms two-word phrases.	Stance fully developed; gait stiff, propulsive, and precipitated; seats himself on child's chair with only fair aim; creeps downstairs backward; has difficulty building tower of three cubes; can throw a ball, but clumsily.

Age in Months	Vocalization and Language	Motor Development
24 to 27	Vocabulary of 300 to 400 words; has two to three-word phases; uses prepositions and pronouns.	Runs but falls when making a sudden turn; can quickly alternate between stance, kneeling or sitting positions; walks stairs up and down, one foot forward only.
30 to 33	Fastest increase in vocabulary; three- to four-word sentences are common; word order, phrase structure, grammatical agreement agreement approximate language of surroundings, but many utterances are unlike anything an adult would say.	Good hand and finger coordination; can move digits independently; manipulation of objects much improved; builds tower of six cubes.
36 to 39	Vocabularly of 1,000 words or more; well-formed sentences using complex grammatical rules, although certain rules have not yet been fully mastered; grammatical mistakes are much less frequent; about 90 per cent comprehensibility.	Runs smoothly with acceleration and deceleration; negotiates sharp and fast curves without difficulty; walks stairs by alternating feet; jumps 12"; can operate tricycle; stands on one foot for a few seconds.

Source: LENNEBERG, E.H., 'The natural history of language'. In: SMITH, F. and MILLER, G.A. (1966) *The Genesis of Language*.

'Babbling and cooing' — early practice

In discussing language at any point in human development it is best to have a clear idea of what we mean by 'language' and what it comprises. Throughout this paper we are concerned solely with speech, i.e. spoken language, as distinct from written language. Speech is pure sound (although if we are near the person speaking we may be able to see his facial expression, body position and gestures, and these may help to convey his meaning). The sounds we hear may be quiet or loud (and learning to make one's speech loud enough or quiet enough is a part of learning to talk). The sounds themselves are described as vowels and consonants, depending on how they are made by the speech organs. Certain syllables and words in an utterance are spoken with more breath force, or stress, than others, i.e. they are 'stressed'. Native speakers automatically learn to place these stresses correctly; it often proves difficult for the non-native speaker of a language to learn to do so. In addition to stress, the pitch, or intonation of words and syllables is also important. Intonation signals something of the mood of the speaker (e.g. whether he is being polite or firm, angry or patient), and whether he is asking a question or making a statement. This patterning of the voice pitch or intonation of an utterance, and the system of stress or varying breath force, are together known as the *prosodic* features of pronunciation.

From the moment he is born, the infant hears language all around him. Even the child separated from his mother in a hospital incubator is talked to and talked about as he is examined, tended, looked at. The child who is with his own mother hears her speech at intervals throughout the day. Mothers vary greatly in the amount of talk they use with very young babies (as with older infants) and with different children within the family, and it is difficult to examine the role of this early language in the child's environment as an element separate from the warmth and care he receives in general. What is clear is that all young babies begin to vocalize whatever the extent or quality of the language and care attending them. This is true even of children born to deaf parents, i.e. born to parents who are unable to hear their children's vocalizations and do not respond vocally to their children. Babies in these circumstances are reported to make as much noise as babies born to hearing families, and to go through the same sequence of development (even though later they learn to respond differentially to deaf and hearing adults).

The newly born child is innately disposed to use his voice to respond to sounds he hears — and it is perhaps in this responsiveness to sound that we should see the real beginnings of language. Certainly there is a response, even on the first day of life, to loud noises (detected in changes in pulse or respiration, or in bodily movements), and within the first weeks there is a response to the human voice. The mother's voice will often sooth a very young crying child. By six months there may be a differentiated response to male and female voices, and to the mother's voice as compared with other female voices. By 11 months children show a marked preference for their mother speaking compared with a stranger speaking, and for mother's normal speech patterns compared with mother speaking abnormally (i.e. without regular intonation and stress). Most mothers would greet such research findings as these with derision as much as to ask 'Well, what would you expect?'. They have, however, quite serious implications: they demonstrate clearly that very young children respond to specific features of speech in a more sophisticated way than might be judged purely from their vocal production. In particular, they show a response to those features of language, intonation and stress, that carry a large amount of meaning.

But the child uses his own voice first of all primarily to express discomfort or comfort. Mothers recognize the message conveyed by their baby's crying and respond accordingly. The difference between these cries can be described in terms of vowels and consonants (or approximations to consonants), the range of sounds gradually changing and being augmented. Some of these are clearly connected with sucking noises, e.g. lip movements which the baby makes in anticipation of sucking produce /m/ or /n/, from whence it is a short step to hunger cries that sound like *mama* or *nana*.

While it is of general interest to look at the inventory of sounds approximating to vowels and consonants produced by the very young baby, it seems especially significant that a key feature of mature speech should also begin to be heard, namely intonation. Some researchers claim to hear the falling intonation pattern (the normal speech tone of statements and assertions) as early as the child's second month. Certainly between 6 and 8 months, intonation is clearly marked. This accompanies the onset of repetitive babbling, long continuous sequences of sounds, many of which — because of the presence of intonational features — sound like fragments of mature speech. This early imitation of intonation or speech tunes should be linked with what was noted a little earlier about the young child's response to normal as distinct from abnormal adult speech.

When the infant begins to coo and babble, he undoubtedly gives a great deal of pleasure to his mother and others around him. He is making sounds which they find pleasant, and producing them in long significant-sounding strings. There is something here that adults begin to recognize as language — or as an approximation to it. But it undoubtedly gives the child pleasure too, and this is the aspect of babbling that is made most of in the literature. It can be compared to a form of play, and certainly there is something exploratory and experimental, as well as self-indulgent, in the child's behaviour. The child enjoys his own activity, the sound of his voice, the things he discovers he can do with it (including starting and stopping, and changes in volume), and the response it often gets from others around him. Their pleasure increases his own pleasure — though the fact that he often indulges in long periods of babbling when no one else is apparently listening points only

to his self-gratification. The child's enjoyment of this, his own performance, is claimed by some to be the root of his subsequent enjoyment of speech and literature. But probably as important as any aesthetic
pleasure is the practice the child gains in making and controlling the
sounds of speech.

Some researchers question the practice element in babbling. They
point to the discontinuity between babbling and true speech behaviour,
the frequent period of silence that intervenes between babbling and the
true onset of speech, and the low take-up in speech of the sounds which
occur most frequently in babbling. This does not necessarily prove that
the practice element in babbling is not significant for the acquisition of
speech; indeed, the practice and control of intonation patterns may be
of more significance than that of speech sounds. What is of undoubted
importance is the child's pleasure in making sounds and using his voice
as such, and — though it is again unproven — in obtaining other people's
response to his performance.

First words

> '. . . . . *Sam (the baby) was of an amicable, endlessly inquiring
> disposition, capable of much sustained experiment. In no time at all
> he'd grown fond of the two large faces that had usurped his world.
> He could even tell them apart — though which of them would appear
> when he howled was still an impenetrable mystery. He knew there
> was a connection between his howling and their appearance, but as
> yet it was a very tenuous one. If only they'd stop poking food into
> him he felt he'd be better able to sort matters out.*
>
> *Then, one might, as he lay in his cot listening to the Chichesters'
> musical snores, the truth flashed upon him. For some time past he'd
> observed that when they desired only to attract his attention, they
> called "Sam!". There was no question of food at all. Therefore:
> "Sam!" he howled delightedly; or, rather, "-am!" as he was still
> rather shaky on his S's. Almost directly the gentler of the two faces
> appeared. It looked intensely excited.*
>
> *"Chichester!" she shouted. "He can talk! He's hungry! He's
> calling for ham!"*

>   (Garfield, *The Sound of Coaches*)

While the adult's response to an infant's babbling is warm and
encouraging, it is even warmer and more encouraging to his first words.
It is an exciting moment when the baby seems to be using words to
express a clear intention — though, as suggested in the quotation here,
the adults may be guessing wildly at the child's meaning. As indicated
on the chart on page 4, isolated 'words', or sounds resembling words

such as *ma, mama, da, ba* are heard from six months onwards, emerging from and blending into the baby's babbling. But between 9 and 12 months a small number of words undoubtedly begin to be used *with meaning.* The vital factor, distinguishing them without any doubt from all the other 'words' or near-words, is that they are said because the child has a meaning to express — or because he is responding to the meaning of other people's speech. He says *Mama* in a variety of circumstances of need and satisfaction, not always to refer to his mother, but increasingly to attract her attention, to mean her and her alone, both when she is present and absent. He learns to say *Shoo!* to send the chickens away, or *Wow-wow* when the dog comes into the room. When he is about to put a piece of paper in his mouth, he desists at the injunction *No!* When his mother says, *Say goodbye to daddy,* he waves his hand.

The child may use different words to indicate the same object. Many of his 'words' are comprehensible only to his mother; it is she who explains that *Baw-baw* means *ball.* In one study 83 per cent of the words used by a 12-month-old child were categorized as 'approximations'. By the time the same child was 18 months old, these had decreased to 56 per cent and a higher proportion of standard words were being used. It is the mother too who interprets words of the child's own invention, and a suprisingly high proportion of his words fall into this category (up to five per cent at 18 months). Thus at this early stage of talking (i.e. from using single words, and on into the period where words are put together) the child is comprehending language and using it to express his own meanings, but in a way that only roughly matches the adult's performance. This seems a strong argument against the explanation that the child acquires language simply by imitation. Imitation certainly plays a role, though to what extent is both ill-defined and disputed. It certainly does not explain the child's performance. 'The infant seems to have caught on to the principles of the communication game long before he can use the standard rules or models presented to him' (Menyuk).

In studies in which researchers have tried to trace the child's acquisition of a word, it has been shown that the child hears the word being used by the mother in various situations before he attempts to reproduce it himself. When he first attempts to say it, it may not be accepted (i.e. understood and responded to by the mother), probably because his version of it is far removed from hers (e.g. /tu/ or /tu-tu/ for *shoe*). Some time later she does accept it, in a situation where the child's meaning is clear (e.g. when he is actually having his shoe put on for him). Later he uses the word when the actual object is not present but when it is again recognized and accepted by his mother or others. Later still his pronunciation matches up to the adult pronunciation of the word. What is not clear is at what stage the child actually acquires the meaning of the word and what that meaning actually is. He seems to pursue his own course, almost regardless of his mother's rejection or acceptance of his use of the new word. To quote Menyuk again, 'It is possible that comprehension of verbal symbols comes about by observation of the use of the symbols in environmental and syntactic contexts and that modification of the production of these symbols also comes about through these means. The game of imitation and correction may be just that — a game which has very little to do with the processes of either comprehension or production . . . . '

One of the commonest features noticed in the young child's use of early words is what has been called *over-extension,* that is, the child uses a word with a wider range of reference than is acceptable for the mature speaker. This is observed across many languages and is thought to be a universal feature of how all children learn meaning, especially from round about 1 year to 2½. An example is the item *bow-wow,* used first to mean a dog, and then to refer to dogs, cows, horses, sheep and cats. Presumably the child perceives certain features such as shape, furriness, four-leggedness, that are common to all the items he incorporates under the word. Later he will learn new words, e.g. *moo,* and set up a new category, diminishing the original one and presumably restructuring his perception of what the word *bow-wow* applies to. It may now, for instance, be applied only to small animals, dogs, cats and sheep. Parents' prompting may help in this process of narrowing down the meaning of a word (e.g. *That's not a dog. It's a cow*), but the accounts in diary-studies of this process do not give the kind of detail which would make a finer analysis possible. The examples of over-extension suggest that children may group items together for a variety of reasons but all apparently related to perceptual categories, e.g. because they seem to serve the same function (box, drawer, bedside table), or because they have the same shape (watch, clocks, all clocks and watches, gas meter, bath scale with round dial, etc.).

A great many of the child's first words are nouns, like *bow-wow, tu-tu, clock,* etc. It may be that naming items that have significance for him in his immediate environment is an important function of language for the child. In a study of the first 50 words learnt by young children, one researcher has shown that nominals, i.e. words referring to objects, people, substances, etc., comprise an average of 50 per cent of the total, while 'specific nominals', words referring to only one person, animal or object (e.g. Mummy, Dizzy — the name of a pet, car — meaning one car in particular) comprise another 14 per cent. But beyond these predictable categories of words, there are also within the first 50 words many that fall into other categories, e.g.

action words : *go, look, up*
modifiers :   *dirty, hot, all-gone, red*
function words (i.e. words that have a grammatical function
        within the sentence) : *what? that?*
personal-social words : *want, please, ouch*

The meaning of a single word utterance is often relatively complex and is understood (most often by the mother) within the whole context in which it is uttered. Thus the word *up* may carry the meaning *Pick me up, Take me upstairs with you, Watch me go up this step*, according to the situation. Similarly *milk* may mean *I want milk, I want some more milk, I've spilt my milk*, etc. The term 'holophrase' was coined to describe these phrase or sentence meanings intended by the single word, and growing attention has been paid to the holophrase in recent years. It is part of the whole issue of how the child learns the meaning of language and learns to convey his meanings through language. This question has often been discussed as if it were only relevant to children at the stage when they 'put words together' and when, therefore, there is a grammatical meaning in their sentences, e.g. *Want up, More milk, Daddy come*. It seems obvious now that the discussion must begin at an earlier stage of language development than the one where the child begins to use sentences and that the interpretation of the child's very first words depends at least on the hearer's syntactical resources.

Putting words together

Over the years (during the late 1950s and early 1960s), the great emphasis in studies of child language has been on the development of grammar. Grammar only becomes possible and analysable when we turn from the single-word utterance to the 'sentence', the utterance of two or more words (the fourth stage in the table given on page 4 above). It is only more recently that attention has been directed to the development of meaning, the child's control of the semantics of language. We need, of course, to look at both and to stress the continuity in terms of the growth of meaning and its syntactical expression from the child's first words — the single-word utterance or holophrase — to the development of his mature control of grammar. Throughout this area of work the influence of Chomsky (referred to in the Introduction) has been great and helps to account for the emphasis on grammar rather than on meaning. Grammars that have appeared in the late 1960s and early 1970s have paid increasing attention to meaning, the way in which language denotes aspects of reality, and in the study of child language relate to the child's expression of meaning. A key feature of all this work has been the meticulous collecting of language from young children and the analysis of this as data valid in itself, i.e. not as immature or imperfect adult speech, but as each child's valid — and systematic — use of language. The child's growing command of language is viewed as a series of systematic approximations to the adult model; these are constantly renewed or replaced by new approximations until maturity is reached.

It is perhaps important to explain the above use of the word *grammar*, as it is central to this discussion. *Grammar* is used here as the descriptive term that is applied to the system of word order and word-endings that relate the parts of any utterance to each other. It is not used in the old-fashioned (schoolbook) prescriptive sense of defining what is acceptable in polite — usually literary — discourse. It can be applied to any dialect or variety of a language. It states what *is*, rather than what *ought* (by some conventions) to be.

The child then, at approximately 18 months, begins 'to put words together' and therefore to develop a first grammar. He says things such as:

> *That box*   *No play*
> *Big boat*   *No a book*
> *Rick go*   *No fall down*
>
> > *See shoe?*   *Want baby*
> > *Truck here?*   *No touch*
> > *Where baby?*   *Have it*

As with the child's one-word utterances earlier, only a limited meaning can be ascribed to these first sentences when they are written down like this or heard out of context. But heard in context, by his mother or by other children and adults who know him well, his first sentences are nearly always understood and interpreted like conventional grammatical sentences. To turn them into the kind of sentences a mature speaker would use, we have to add the grammatical apparatus that characterizes mature speech, i.e. the grammatical words or functors (articles, auxiliary or modal verbs, pronouns, etc.) and the word-endings or inflections, that show some of the internal relationships within an utterance. It is the omission of these features (not entirely consistently as can be seen from the above examples) that has led to the description of this stage of speech as 'telegraphic'. The meaning, as in a telegram, is carried largely by nouns, verbs, and adjectives, the 'content' words of the language. Like the child's one-word utterances, these early sentences convey a variety of meanings. These have been classified in various ways. The actions that accompany them and the intonation with which they are spoken are also clues here. Thus, it is fairly straightforward to characterize:

	Big boat	as declarative	*(That's a big boat)*
	No play	as negative	*(I'm not playing)*
	See shoe?	as a question	*(Do you see my shoe?)*
and	*Want baby*	as imperative	*(Give me the baby)*

The prosodic features of both stress and intonation are indeed of crucial importance in indicating further differentiation of meaning. Thus the same child is described as saying *'Christy room,* with stress on *Christy,* which indicates posssession (Christy's room), and the same utterance with stress on the second word, *Christy 'room,* which suggests some meaning related to location and thus to a prepositional use (Christy's in the room).

Indeed, as suggested earlier, from the child's earliest experience of language, it is obvious that stress and intonation are extremely important. One of the theories as to why the child's first sentences are telegraphic in the way described here also relates to these prosodic features of speech. It is precisely the nouns, verbs and adjectives, the content words, that carry the main stress and are heard most clearly in adult speech. In words of more than one syllable, young children are often heard to miss out some of the unstressed syllables, again almost as though they did not hear them. Thus they may say *'raff for giraffe,* or *'pression for expression.* Apart from this, a telegraphic form of English does in fact communicate quite well. The missing function words can often be guessed (as in reading a telegram). Researchers have also pointed out how parents do in any case repeat many nouns, verbs and adjectives as single isolated words, often simply to teach their meaning (*doggie; jump; dirty*). All of these seem good reason for the child's first sentences being in this form.

It is perhaps obvious — but also noteworthy — that the word order of the telegraphic sentence, again like that of the adult telegram, preserves the word order of the mature untelegraphic sentence. This must relate to the mature sentences the child himself hears all around him, and helps the adult to understand the child's utterances. Word order is an important feature of English grammar, distinguishing, for instance, the subject of a sentence from the direct object, and both subject and direct object from indirect object. 'It is conceivable that the child 'intends' the meanings coded by his word orders and that, when he preserves the order of an adult sentence, he does so because he wants to say what the order says. It is also possible that he preserves word order just because his brain works that way and that he has no comprehension of the semantic contrasts involved' (Brown and Bellugi, 1964).

As the child learns more — and the process is very rapid from 18 months onwards — so the length of his utterances increases. But length does not consist simply of longer and longer strings of words; it lies in the complexity of words and parts of words, the grammatical morphemes (or inflections) that shortly begin to fill out the telegraphic style of the very earliest sentences. (The 'Mean Length of Utterance' or 'MLU' is used as a standard and reliable marker of linguistic maturity up to about the age of four; it is arrived at by counting the total number of morphemes, i.e. the minimum meaningful units, in any corpus of language being examined, and dividing the total by the number of 'sentences' within the corpus.) A convenient way of illustrating this kind of development is to trace the development of the two-word (all two-morpheme) sentences given above. The noun phrases and verb forms of the original sentences are illustrated at an in-between stage of development, and at a later stage when they match more or less perfectly.

Stages in the development of declarative, negative, question and imperative sentences

	A Early	B In Between	C Later
Declarative	*That box* *Big boat* *Rick go*	*That's box* *That big boat* *Rick going*	*That's a box* *That's a big boat* *Rick is going*
Negative	*No play* *No a book* *No fall down*	*I no play* *That not book* *(a) I not falling down* *(b) I'm not fall down*	*I won't play* *That's not a book* *I'm not falling down*
Question	*See shoe?* *Truck here?* *Where baby?*	*Mommy see shoe?* *Truck's here?* *(a) Where baby is?* *(b) Where's baby is?*	*Do you see the shoe?* *Is the truck here?* *Where's the baby?*
Imperative	*Want baby!* *No touch!* *Have it!*		*I want the baby*, or *Give me the baby!* *Don't touch it!* *Give it to me!*

Source: MENYUK, Paula (1971), *The Acquisition and Development of Language*, Prentice-Hall.

The sentences in the 'in-between' stage show development from the earliest ones, but still lack some of the features of a mature speaker's sentences. At the in-between stage a grammatical subject is introduced (*big boat* has become *that big boat* 'that's a big boat'; *no play* has become *I no play*; *see shoe?* has become *Mommy see shoe?*). The verb forms have expanded and include auxiliary verbs (*I'm no fall ...*) and some inflections (*I not falling down*). By the later stage there is a range of pronouns, negatives and modal verbs (*I won't play*), and word order in questions has become fully acceptable as a mature form (*Where baby is?* has become *Where's the baby?*).

There are of course considerable variations in different children in the rate at which the immature 'baby-language' sentences develop into those with the grammar of the mature speaker. Perhaps the most interesting feature of this development is not the rate at which it takes place so much as the similarity in the sequence of development observed in all children whose language has been collected and described. The finer analysis of the sequence of development, moreover, illustrates very clearly the process by which young children learn the rules of language. Grammatical rules are not suddenly learnt; from the day the child first uses a new form from time to time in his speech (e.g. the final /s/ and /z/ sound in the majority of noun plurals), to the day when he uses it more or less whenever it is required, there is usually a long period. One child is described as having no plural /s/ or /z/ marker in his speech at all at 19 months; then for the next three months he used it from time to time, a total of 15 per cent of all the instances where a mature speaker would have used it. During this period he could be described as learning the rule that /s/ and /z/ are added to certain nouns when they have a plural meaning. In this period too, the rule was never mis-applied. Then came a period when he used /s/ and /z/ plural forms of nouns very often correctly, but quite often in instances where they were not needed (*that my shoes*, speaking of one shoe only) — here the rule was over-learnt. Finally came a period when it was applied correctly 90 per cent of the time. A similar sequence of learning, including the period of over-generalization can be traced for other forms, and indeed the literature, like the everyday anecdotes indulged in by all parents of young children, is full of examples of over-generalized rules, of children saying *foots* instead of *feet*, *goed* instead of *went*, *mines* instead of *mine*. Eventually the over-generalizations disappear, but the fact that they occur, and occur systematically, gives striking support to the basic hypothesis that language acquisition is the learning of rules which enable the child and adult alike to generate limitless sentences which they have not heard spoken by anyone else.

The process of language acquisition will continue throughout childhood and into adolescence, but all later development can be called an increasing familiarity with the refinements of linguistic structure rather than new basic language learning. It is of course linked with the child's conceptual development, and hard — or impossible — to say that some difficulties are purely linguistic or purely conceptual. The child's understanding and use of spatial terms, for instance, may be a slower process than has often been thought from simply observing that he uses them in apparently appropriate contexts. The pre-school child's responses to instructions containing *more* may be correct in the adult sense; but his responses to similar instructions containing *less* may be identical to those containing *more*. There are often difficulties over adjectives like *big* and *small*, *tall* and *short*. Specific tests of comprehension of prepositions reveal similar deviations and fluctuations in children aged three to five. A study of children aged five and upwards showed that there are some structures (e.g. containing the verbs *promise*, *ask* and *tell*) in which children at least up to the age of eight find great difficulty. It may well be that a fuller understanding of these later stages in the child's growth to linguistic maturity would help teachers and others to modify the language they use and enable children to participate more fully in the language of school.

Chapter Two

The Mother's Role

A baby usually receives close attention from his mother, and from birth is responsive to her. Bruner calls this the child's *social responsiveness*, and in it lies the motivation to speech. For this reason it seems clear that research into mother–child interactions in early infancy may have important bearing on our knowledge of language acquisition. Modern technology has enabled workers in this field to develop new methods of observation and of analysis of the data including frame-by-frame analysis of film and videotape, and several ongoing studies seem particularly relevant to the present report. For instance, a study of the characteristics of mother and infant vocal interactions shows there is a greater reciprocity – or mutual responsiveness – in these than casual observation might reveal. A mother and her baby rarely vocalize at the same time: they take it in turns, responding to one another like partners in a conversation. The timing is thought to depend on the mother's sensitivity, as she paces herself by the baby's vocalizations. The same kind of response, i.e. the mother taking her cues from the baby, has been observed when the two look at various toys in turn. Up until the end of the first year, the baby's behaviour determines the mother's responses. Her responses are thought to be crucial in the baby's development.

It is as if there is a continuum of 'fostering behaviour' on the part of the mother, from the baby's earliest days and on through its development of speech. Indeed, some researchers argue that the quality of the child's language development depends on the degree of successful communication it has had with an adult since birth. Bruner's work at Oxford is an attempt to link the baby's pre-linguistic learning with language acquisition more explicitly: in the child's interaction with his mother he learns certain fundamental concepts for regulating joint action and ways of directing his attention. Bruner defines some of these concepts as agent, action, object, location, linked with a topic on which comments (i.e. relating to agent, action, etc.) are made. These concepts remind us of the recent grammars referred to earlier that isolate features of language under these same headings, rather like the *cases* in traditional grammars.) These, says Bruner, are the features of meaning which appear in the infant's early sentences, as his language develops in contexts in which he and his mother share and in which they both attend to some aspect of behaviour or the environment.

It looks as if these detailed analyses of mother–child interaction in the first years of life will eventually specify the features of that inter- action which have most significance for the child's subsequent develop- ment. It had long been observed that the child who lacked a mother's close attention usually suffered developmentally, but the precise nature of the significant features in mother–child behaviour have not been explored.

Mothers vary greatly in the way they respond to their babies. Some talk far more than others; some are nearly silent. There is what might be described as a greater natural warmth in the behaviour of some. In spite of these and other differences in the environment, the infant's *potential* for language seems unaffected. It may develop late, or more slowly, but it *will* develop. The onset of speech seems in fact to be remarkably unaffected by such factors as whether the child is a first or second child in the family. But there are differences in the nature and quality of the child's early speech. Unintelligibility seems to occur more commonly in second and subsequent children than in the first. Children reared in orphanages are often below average in speech as in motor development. Whatever the importance of the child's inter- action with other children in his speech development, it is obviously the quality and extent of his verbal and social interaction with his mother, or mother substitute, that has the greatest significance.

In terms of the mother's response to the child who has begun to speak, there is already a great deal of observational and experimental research. This has accompanied the collecting of data described in the previous section. The person to whom the one- or two-year-old addresses most of his early utterances is usually the mother; often the only person who understands most of them is again the mother. An important point about the child's one-word sentences, and then about his 'telegraphic' speech, with its omissions and idiosyncratic lexicon, is that these features do not impede communication. The mother is in the same situation with the child, familiar with his development so far and his stock of knowledge: thus, as far as one can judge, she under- stands even the incomplete sentence. Why then does the child continu- ally improve upon his language? (It is worth pointing out that many of the features of grammar that he omits from his telegraphic speech such as inflections, plural-markers, and even auxiliary verbs, are redun- dant features of language. The speaker's intentions are often clear without them, as the same meaning may be signalled by several differ- ent features in the sentence, e.g. if you say *two dogs*, *two* is sufficient indication of plurality without the additional *-s* on the noun.)

There seems to be something that drives the infant on to match his speech forms to those of the other speakers around him. Does his mother's behaviour play a role in this? One of the accepted beliefs about child language was that parents helped by correcting the child's 'ungrammatical' utterances and by modelling acceptable ones that he imitated. In fact the detailed observational studies of the last fifteen years show that parents normally pay little or no attention to children's grammar, and do not usually correct it. Direct imitation of 'correct' forms, offered as a model by parents as a substitute for 'incorrect' ones, rarely occurs. The child's ability then to handle and develop grammar develops with little or no deliberate attention from his mother. If she does 'correct' him, it tends to be a correction of the truth or accuracy of what he is saying, i.e. a correction of the content rather than the form. It is often as though she does not hear his immature grammar as she responds to the meaning of his utterance. Anecdotal examples of parents trying to correct immaturities in their children's speech show that the child too is concerned with content not form, and cannot be diverted from the one to the other. The mother may deliberately offer a 'correct' grammatical form for the child to imitate in her own speech:

She said, *My teacher holded the baby rabbits and we patted them.*
I asked, *Did you say your teacher held the baby rabbits?*
She answered, *Yes.*
I then asked, *What did you say she did?*
She answered again, *She holded the baby rabbits and we patted them.*
Did you say she held them tightly? I asked.
No, she answered, *She holded them loosely.*

But this process clearly does not work very well. Neither does a more obvious correction:

Child: *Nobody don't like me.*
Parent: *No, say 'Nobody likes me'.*
Child: *Nobody don't like me.*
         (eight repetitions of this dialogue)
Parent: *No. Now listen carefully; say 'Nobody likes me'.*
Child: *Oh! Nobody don't likes me!*

If the new rule is not yet part of the child's grammatical competence, then it does not look as if it can be suddenly introduced into it through the child being offered the chance to imitate a different model.

It was also thought that the child might learn to reject immature, 'incorrect' forms, and to consolidate his learning of mature ones, through the selectiveness of his parents' response, i.e. that there was a more positive, approving response to some of his utterances, and a more disapproving response to others. Again, the studies show no variation in responses that can be clarified in this way. The mother's approval or disapproval is of the truth value of what the child has said rather than the form in which he has said it. She may correct pronunciation or disapprove of a 'naughty' word, but she does not seem to hear that the child has said, 'Why the dog won't eat?' instead of, 'Why won't the dog eat?'.

What then does the mother do that positively contributes to the child's language development? We have talked of her responsiveness in both the child's pre-linguistic and linguistic stages, and her attention to his meanings. All this is part of her general concern for the child and his development. She and other adults take pleasure in his development, in each manifestation of it, and identify and encourage new modes of behaviour — and growth in language. Intuitively, it seems, mothers talk to their babies in a consistent and fairly predictable way. They do in fact use 'baby-talk', a kind of talk that is not necessarily characterized by babywords like *doggie* or *horsie,* but by features which seem deliberately to assist the child's language learning. The mother matches her speech to the needs of the child. Her utterances are very short when the child is still a young baby; later they become longer. As well as being short, they are grammatically simple. They contain many concrete nouns, diminutives and terms of endearment. Thus, in terms of grammar, the mother's speech provides a consistently simple model. In terms of function, it encourages and stimulates the child's responsiveness. It is a teaching language, at first singling out aspects of the environment she wants the child to respond to. Often she asks questions and provides the answers immediately afterwards. (In so doing she may unconsciously be showing the child how to make a conversation). Later, her language serves the function of socialization, more and more obviously influencing the child's behaviour and his reactions — her own reactions are often exaggerated in her speech and the frequency of her voice is raised.

Perhaps the feature of the mother's language that has received most attention in the literature is the way in which she repeats a great many of the child's own utterances, usually in an 'expanded' version, that is, in a form which adds something to the original. The child's telegraphic speech is thus expanded in the mother's responses into the fully grammatical forms of adult speech:

Child	Mother
Baby highchair	*Baby is in the highchair*

Mummy eggnog	*Mummy had her eggnog.*
Eve lunch	*Eve is having lunch.*
Mummy sandwich	*Mummy'll have a sandwich.*
Sat wall	*He sat on the wall.*
Throw Daddy	*Throw it to Daddy.*
Pick glove	*Pick the glove up.*

It has been shown that some mothers respond to their children's speech with expansions like these for more than 30 per cent of the time. (It has been suggested that adults seem to imitate children more often than children imitate adults.) The mother's sentences preserve the word order of the child's, but add the functors, or grammatical words, and inflections. The child's meaning is taken for granted. It is simply expressed in the form of mature adult speech. From the point of view of the mother, it seems to serve more or less as a kind of confirmation of what the child wants to communicate. Perhaps, too, if other adults are present, the mother is also re-processing the child's speech for their benefit, giving a kind of clarification, knowing as she does that no other adult knows the meanings her child wishes to convey as well as she herself does.

The mother's expansions, it has been suggested, may be a powerful force in teaching the young child the grammar of the language and thus the means of encoding more precisely the relationships of time, number, location, etc., which are expressed by these means. An alternative hypothesis is that the child learns grammar from the normal flow of adult or mature speech that is addressed to him, or is heard by him, throughout the day. The mother's expansions are only a part of this. An experiment designed to see if the effect of expansions on children's language could be separated from the effect of sheer quantity of well-informed speech did not really provide anything conclusive on this score, partly because the experimental conditions could not replicate the home situation of the children involved. Moreover, as soon as a situation is set up in which an aspect of language is isolated for special treatment, so many other factors are involved (e.g. the distortion of the child's usual conversational relationship with the adult) that the results are fairly meaningless. Another experiment contrasted mother's *expansions* with *extensions* of their children's speech, an extension being defined as sections of discourse where the adult maintains the topic raised by the child, adding to it, commenting or elaborating on it, and thus employing related vocabulary and concepts across several sentences, e.g.

Child	**Adult's Expansion:**
Dog bark	*Yes, the dog is barking.*

Adult's Extension:
Yes, but he won't bite. He's a nice dog.

In the study in question, it looks as if the adult's extensions have a more positive effect on the development of the child's language than expansions in effecting the mean length of utterance, the complexity of the verb form, etc. It is suggested that the general richness of verbal stimulation — a factor incidentally which sustains the focus on meaning rather than form — is the critical variable. Certainly this seems a better way of sustaining the child's attention and motivation than the comparatively limiting use of expansions only.

Another feature of mothers' and adults' language in talking to young children is what we might call its formulaic quality. Many of the formulas used with young children are heard in few other contexts (e.g. 'Who's a good boy, then?'). The repetition — often with a special intonation — of expressions like *Bye-bye, Night-night,* of rhyming expressions, and of nonsense words and nursery rhymes, would again come into this category. Whether they contribute to the child's learning of phonology is hard to say. What they do seem to contribute to is the encouragement of his sense of pleasure in language, to his listening to the surface 'sounds' of language and thus perhaps to the basis of a metalinguistic awareness — i.e. an awareness of what language is in itself — that may be important in the development later of reading and writing skills.

In providing young children with formulas, rhymes, and rituals ('What does the dog say? What does the duck say? What does the cat say?' etc.) the mother is encouraging repetitious behaviour. Children take great pleasure in this kind of verbal play, often it seems for the response they get from adults who admire their cleverness, often for some purely personal pleasure in the act of repetition itself. It would appear that this is related to the pre-sleep monologues of young children, monologues in which it is conjectured there is a trying out of newly acquired grammatical forms and of sound play:

> (2 year old boy) — *Bobo's not throwing*
> *Bobo can throw*
> *Bobo can throw it*
> *Bobo can throw*
> *Oh Oh*
> *Go go go.*

Such exercises have been called variations on a theme rather than repetitions as such. They may be the child's attempts to hear what he can and what he cannot do with the words at his disposal. Repetitions generated by the child himself may serve some important cognitive function. Repetitive behaviour is said to be frequently the outward manifestation of an emerging cognitive ability, an ability that the child needs to realize through some form of action. Not unrelated to this is the fact that one of the child's earliest words is *Again!* used as a demand for adults to repeat not only physical games, but rhymes and songs and other verbal rituals. Fun as these may be, they also seem to serve several very specific purposes in the child's social and linguistic development.

Although mothers may to some extent model their behaviour on that of their own parents, or on that of other mothers, it looks very much as though the way they talk to their babies is instinctive. (It has, incidentally, been observed that quite young children of four or five modify their own speech when talking to younger children, just as they change it again when talking to older people, or to adults in different roles.) We have seen that the mother, in talking to her young child, tends to use short, grammatically simple utterances, many terms of endearment and diminutives and concrete nouns, and that much of it is language which stimulates the child's responsiveness, helping him to focus on things around him, asking him questions, and often providing the answers. We have also noted the way the mother's speech responds to what the child himself has said, expanding it grammatically, and often extending its reference. Her speech may also contain many formulas, rhyming expressions and nonsense words, which seem to generate the child's pleasure in using and responding to these features of language.

The mother then is not simply fostering the child's language, in terms of his control of grammar, the extent of his vocabulary, and the accuracy of his pronunciation. She fosters his pleasure in language; she also fosters something we can best call *the functions language serves in the child's life.* It has often been said that language is what language does, and this has taken on more meaning in recent years as the attention of linguists and psychologists has turned increasingly to describing language function. An examination of language function is in fact the necessary prerequisite for any serious work on intervention in children's language education (and as such forms a substantial part of the argument of the next chapter). For the moment, however, it is useful to look at the way in which the mother fosters this aspect of her child's language.

Most of the research in this area looks at children aged three upwards and their verbal interaction with their mothers. However, there is evidence which suggests that well before the age of three children learn some language functions more than others. Even when the child is still at the stage of using single words, his mother's interaction with him seems to be directing language more towards some funtions than others. For instance, the two-year-old is not simply naming in his one-word utterances:

'In terms of the function of language, one child seems to be learning to talk about things and the other about self and other people; one is learning an object language, one a social interaction language' (Nelson, 1973).

All the children in this study by Katherine Nelson had acquired 50 words by 24 months but some were already learning a more *referential* use of language, largely 'object-oriented'; others were using a more expressive, 'self-oriented', use of language. The referential language-users were slower in using speech units of two words or more than the expressive language-users. The perceived function of language seemed to influence its content and the growth of its complexity from the very earliest stage.

In the same study the author singles out the mother who responds enthusiastically to her child's talk, but who at the same time allows the child to set the pace, to use toys and words in her own way — and thus to develop her own meanings:

Mother:	*Is that a car?*
Jane:	*Bah*
Mother:	*Yes, car. Here's another car.*
Jane:	*Gah.*
Mother:	*Car, yes.*
Jane:	*Bah, Daddy.*
Mother:	*Daddy. Daddy's car is all gone.*

The mother accepts the child's words even when they seem incorrect to others. But some mothers seem to exercise much more control over the learning situation and reject many of the child's attempts at speaking instead of picking them up like Jane's mother in the above example. Another finding in the same study is that where a mother's speech is very directive, there seems to be a negative effect on the development of the child's language.

It is obviously much more difficult to describe the role the mother plays in conversations like those quoted here, and to analyse the child's growing awareness of language function, than it is to analyse the formal features of language. However, studies like Katherine Nelson's begin to provide a basis for this kind of work, and in England, Joan Tough's work with older children — to be looked at more closely in the next chapter — is undoubtedly going to be important for parents and their children, for educationists and linguists alike, for some time to come.

Recent work in socio-linguistics provides a useful theoretical statement about this key area in the study of language acquisition:

'The acquisition of competency for use, indeed, can be stated in the same terms as the acquisition of competence for grammar. Within the development matrix in which knowledge of the sentences of a language is acquired, children also acquire knowledge of a set of ways in which sentences are used. From a finite experience of speech acts and their interdependence with socio-cultural features they develop a general theory of the speaking appropriate in their community, which they employ, like other forms of tacit cultural knowledge (competence) in conducting and interpreting social life' (Hymes, 1970).

Children have to learn the functions of language through a process of social interaction, and the mother's role in this early learning is obviously crucial.

Chapter Three

Intervention in Language Development

The present decade in education has been marked both by a steadily growing interest in early education – with government policy apparently designed to encourage growth and consolidation in pre-school provision – and by an intensification of academic interest in language and its role in education. Both of these interests are linked to a world-wide concern with poverty and inequality, and the startling differences in living standards and opportunities which are to be found within and between different countries. Rich nations are seen to have a responsibility to poorer ones; successful groups in society are seen to have a responsibility for improving the lot of the unsuccessful. The unsuccessful, which in this debate largely means those of low socioeconomic status, must be helped to break out of the vicious circle of imprisoning causes and effects: poverty, low educational achievement, poor job expectations, substandard housing, etc.

In one way or another, language is seen to play an important role in improving the situation. For members of minority groups who do not speak the language of the majority, or who speak a non-standard variety deemed to many to be not simply non-standard but sub-standard, language education may open the door to more effective communication with peers and superiors, it may provide access to better qualifications or better jobs, and it may lead to great improvement in the learner's life-style. For native speakers of the standard dialect – and the debate till now has largely been about English in the United States and in Britain – greater facility in the use of language, and in having access to a wider range of language functions, should make for school success or, for adults, for more control over one's own destiny. It is in this context, then, that we pick up the issue of intervention in the language development of young children.

The questions that hang over what it is in the mother's behaviour that really fosters the infant's development of language, hang also – and more perplexingly – over what it is that other adults can do to foster the same process. We must also be concerned with where, if anywhere, intervention can best take place and what form it should take. The mother's role in the child's language development seems largely to be an intuitive one. The moments when she sees herself as deliberately 'teaching' her child language are comparatively few. In total we know very little about the things she does which specifically facilitate the child's learning of language. But what we *do* know is that there are differences — many of which have been extensively described — between the way children end up using language. In the last section of the preceding chapter it was suggested that these differences begin to show at a very early age, even when children are only using one-word utterances. By the age of two they have begun to learn not just language, but ways of using it. Some of these ways are more restrictive than others, and in the long term the restrictiveness is bound to relate to educational success.

This has become particularly clear in the most recent work of Dr Tough and her associates on the language used by children aged three upwards. This work begins to make educational sense within a debate that has gone on for much longer and which has been particularly perplexing for those concerned with early education. The main stimulus had for long been the work of Basil Bernstein, and in particular his theory of language codes which he developed out of the analysis of language used by parents and children in different socioeconomic groups. Much of this analysis was concentrated on the formal features of language. Berstein established the concepts of 'elaborated' and 'restricted' codes, and first offered descriptions of them in terms of sentence length, grammatical complexity, extent of vocabulary, etc. As he developed his theory, he was able to base it on a much broader concept than one linked only to surface features of language. He related the notion of elaborated and restricted codes not simply to the way in which language is used to encode experience, but to the family organization itself and the way individuals within it interact with one another and exert control over one another.

The notion of elaborated and restricted codes is still a useful one to explore in looking at different ways of using language. From a fairly early stage Berstein had suggested that the potential for an elaborated coding and for a restricted coding are there all the time but that some people preponderantly make use of one type more than the other. (This is very different from the popular version of his theory which seems to state that people in some groups use one code, and others the other.) The essential difference between the two is in the kind of reference that is made and the way this is related to the immediate situation or context. With some speakers, the hearer cannot make sense of what he is saying unless he is there in the situation with him and in all likelihood shares his background of reference. This is in fact a limited, restricted use of language, much used by people who share similar backgrounds and interests and are conversing in informal situations. An elaborated use of language is relatively context-free, 'universal', available in a wider sense. For this purpose, the form of language used is essentially more formal, drawing on syntactical devices to express explicit relationships (cause and effect, concession, time, etc.) and thus likely to be grammatically more complex than language used in the restricted sense.

Within the elaborated use of language by middle class children, there is a constant function of language — again reflecting an acquired 'habit' of mind — in its use as an instrument of analysis and synthesis in problem solving.

> *'In lower class discourse, mothers more often order, or please, or complain, than set up a problem or give feedback. Such usage possibly accounts for the 'poor reinforcement value' of verbal reactions by parents of less advantaged children: language is not usually used for signalling outcome or hailing good tries. What is most lacking in the less advantaged mother's use of language is analysis-and-synthesis: the dissection of relevant features in a task and their appropriate recombinings in terms of connection, cause-and-effect, and so on' (Bruner, 1975).*

It is the different ways in which meanings are handled and explored by the speaker that are really at the heart of the concept of restricted versus elaborated codes. Broadly speaking, educational success seems to depend on children learning to use an elaborated code.

It is unfortunate that Berstein's terms 'elaborated' and 'restricted' have been adopted in a superficial way to describe differences in language. It is the abuse of his theory, rather than an attempt to grapple with its complexity, that has led to the castigation of Berstein and other researchers in recent years. Having set up a simple pair of labels, it has been tempting to pin them indiscriminately onto children and in turn to relate them to value judgments: restricted means bad, elaborated means good. It has also been tempting to confuse Berstein's *codes* with *dialects,* and to dismiss non-standard forms of English (both of pronunciation and grammar) as bad and needing to be changed to standard forms. This has been a particularly important debate in the United States where the low achievement of black children has focused attention on their educational needs, and where one of these has been identified as failure to perform adequately in standard American English. In all likelihood the average American teacher has been no better informed about dialects than the average British teacher; it has probably been a long-standing aim of most educational systems to obliterate non-standard dialects and get all pupils to perform in standard English. However, in America the debate has been sharpened by the contribution of socio-linguists like Labov and Shuy who have developed tools for the rigorous description of non-standard dialects, particularly Black English, and demonstrated both their formal status as varieties of language (i.e. as adequate in grammatical and lexical resources as the standard dialect to serve any purpose) and their flexibility in serving whatever range of functions users might wish to put them to. The fact that logical treatises are not written in dialect does not mean that dialect could not be used for this purpose if a writer — and an agreed upon written form — were to hand.

Behind the debate about dialect, and indeed about language codes, is of course a debate about people. The latest 'political-educational' writers, drawing fairly freely on Labov, defend the dialect speakers, the under-privileged, the poor, who are not only described as lacking in some language skills, compared with their more favoured peers, but as lacking language altogether and the cultural experiences which it partly transmits. They realize that attempts to do something to remedy this situation can easily become attacks on the child and his background. If the home is the most influential force in developing his early language, then the home itself comes under attack when his failings are pointed out. Teachers and others tread a razor's edge between intervening and interfering, diagnosing, judging and being seen to condemn.

There is a current anxiety that the values and cultures of different communities and different homes should not be devalued by the school and other forms of educational provision. In this anxiety it is easy to lose sight of the evidence that gave rise to much of the new thinking (which in turn stimulated more research). For instance, one of the earliest and most influential studies in this area was conducted in America and looked at the mother-child interaction in a number of black and white families of high and low socioeconomic status. This is the famous Hess and Shipman study which coined the probably over-used paradox 'the meaning of deprivation is a deprivation of meaning', referring to the limitations built into the cognitive environment of a home — and therefore into the early cognitive development of children from that home — where behaviour tends to be controlled by rules that relate to the individual's status rather than to the characteristics of the individual situation. The interaction situations dealt with in this study were basically tasks in which the mother worked in one way or another with her child (e.g. sorting toys or blocks). Maternal teaching styles were found to vary greatly between the families of high and low socio-economic status. Mothers of upper class status families tended to be person-orientated, explaining tasks more fully, providing a wider frame of reference for the child, and taking more aspects of the total situation into account. The status-orientated mothers defined the child's role as passive and compliant, and gave a generally much more restricted and simplified message. Although the same study analyses the language used in these situations in terms of sentence length, structural complexity, etc., it is of course the functional aspect that is of most signficance together with the relation of this to the cognitive environment that is seen to be reflected in the interactions.

While there are several British studies which like that of Hess and Shipman develop the ideas of Basil Berstein, the most influential work in Britain is undoubtedly the longitudinal study by Dr Tough, referred to above. It again compares children from linguistically disadvantaged homes with those from advantaged homes and has produced results which indicate very clear differences in the functions children have learnt for language by the time they are three years old. Dr Tough's study is not in fact an analysis of mother-child interaction, but relates data from recordings of children's spontaneous use of language to interview material obtained from their mothers. While the structural analysis of the children's language shows that generally there is a significantly higher degree of complexity in that of the advantaged children, this is not in itself thought to be important unless it can be shown to reflect differences in the kinds of meaning expressed. Such differences have been found:

> *'All the children in both groups used language to maintain their own status, rights and property and for threats and criticism of others. But, and this appears to be the important issue, the children in the advantaged groups used language more frequently for recall, to make associations, to analyse details, to make a synthesis, to anticipate and predict, to collaborate and plan, to give explanations and to project through the imagination, to hypothesize and approach logical reasoning' (Tough, 1974).*

The same children's language was recorded at five and a half and seven and a half, and an important fact that seems to emerge is not that the children in the disadvantaged group fail to develop the language functions listed above, but that they develop them later than the children in the advantaged group. In other words, there is a time lag. It is suggested that the change in the children's experience of language when they come to school may promote the development of uses which the home experience has so far failed to promote. Until the full report of this study is available, we have little information about the different language backgrounds of the two groups of children, but the reports that are available indicate differences in the language-fostering environments of the homes:

> *'First, it is clear that talk went on in all the homes and that the children were engaged in it at some time. All the mothers talked*

freely to us and it is unlikely that they were silent in their own homes. Both at three and at seven it seemed that all children asked questions and most mothers tried to answer them. But the mothers of the disadvantaged group indicated that they either had not the resources or the patience to give satisfactory anwers . . . . Many of the children in the disadvantaged group were reported as spending much of the day playing outside in the company of other pre-school children. The advantaged three-year-olds on the other hand were reported as rarely out of sight and sound of some adult, and it seems likely that they were therefore more frequently in talk with the adult' (Tough, 1974).

The conclusions of this study support those of Hess and Shipman, and Bernstein and his associates, about the different teaching styles of different homes, the way in which mothers view the use of toys, the mothers' views of the purposes language serves, and the way in which they seek to control their children. The central experience clearly emerges as the adult-child dialogue; differences in the quality and functions of this dialogue radically affect the child's own language development, his use of language and his development of meaning:

'The dialogue with the adult is important then for two reasons. First, it provides a model on which the child can base his inner activity of thinking, and second, it gives the child the help he needs to learn the alternating inwards-outwards switching from reflection to projection which enables him to meet the requirements of dialogue' (Tough, 1974).

Dr Tough's conclusions have obvious and important implications for those considering the form intervention should take in the young child's language education. This is discussed in the following section.

Pre-school language work

The Plowden report in this country, and the Coleman report in America, document the nature — and to some extent the causes — of educational disadvantage. Both documents suggest positive action for attempting to remedy the situations they describe. Both are sometimes blamed for establishing the official belief that the failure of many children at school is basically the failure of the home (though both have a great deal to say about the deficiencies of schools themselves). Both of course are key documents in defining policies of educational intervention, that is, of intervening in the child's early learning at school in order to render the disadvantaged child less disadvantaged.

American work in this field has some considerable value in this discussion, both because it is extensive and varied (representing a much greater federal and state expenditure than could be feasible in Britain), and also because in many ways it has influenced both attitudes and practice in this country. British literature on the topic tends to be more guarded than the American in defining this role for nursery education, and indeed, in defining the 'failings' of the home. It is also more guarded, or simply less explicit, in defining the objectives of nursery education in general and special aims that nursery education might have for disadvantaged children. Although literature about nursery education has practically always paid a passing tribute to the 'child's linguistic development', it is in fact only in very recent years that the issue of language in early education in Britain has been really well ventilated. But the key, perhaps, to the distinctions that may be drawn between American and British work in this field is in the word *programmes*. On the whole, American education, from pre-school to university level, is characterized by being explicit about aims and objectives, curricula and methods. This drive to be explicit leads to the creation of syllabuses and programmes, i.e. to very detailed statements about the curriculum that often seem both directive and over-generalized, in the sense that they apparently leave little leeway for the different needs of the individual pupil, or for teachers' individuality, to operate. In early childhood education in particular, this approach seems to have a formality which in many ways conflicts with the freer, child-centred philosophy which is so highly valued in Britain. The large-scale federal funding of projects under various Acts in the 1960s, designed to reduce social inequality in America, has also helped promote the idea of *programmes* in education. Of these, the Head Start Programme is the best known. Obviously, a programme can mean different things in different situations, but it is a plan for a carefully thought-out course of action, staffed, timed and often worked out in great detail in terms of what is taught and when. If American education is characterized by too great a faith in programmes, it might be thought that British education is characterized by too great a distrust of them and what they imply for the direction of teachers' behaviour.

It is of course virtually impossible to conduct a programme aimed solely at improving children's language skills. The interrelation of language and cognition means that the majority of the programmes relevant to this study are programmes directed at both cognitive and linguistic skills. Moreover, the enrichment of experience, and the relationship of experience to growth in language and motivation in general, has obviously concerned educationists in America as it has here. Thus, if one looks at the whole spectrum of intervention programmes, they can be seen to range from those with an emphasis on the enrichment of experience, 'Montessori methods', play and social interaction, to those which emphasize structured activities, designed to promote cognitive development accompanied by the appropriate linguistic expression. Some considerable arguments, based on observation of child-rearing and class differences, are used to justify the need for some specifically structured activities rather than an all-round enriching of the experience provided.

Although there are many reasons for rejecting the highly structured programmes of Bereiter and Engelman, it does seem that structured programmes as a whole are more successful than other types in raising children's scores on tests of intelligence and language, especially for those children we have here called disadvantaged. Bereiter and Engelman's best known work is structured in the sense of having very specific language goals which are meant to be arrived at by precise drill and repetitive methods, with correct behaviour being rewarded in various ways and incorrect behaviour punished. Few other American programmes are as extreme. For example, some focus on processes of problem solving, without laying down the specific vocabulary and sentence patterns that are to be used in the process. Others emphasize general vocabulary development through the learning of names of objects and attributes portrayed in certain provided materials but using group discussion rather than drill as the method. Yet others lay more emphasis on social interaction, especially on children engaging in communication tasks with one another in the course of which they draw on their own linguistic resources, but for which they may need to learn new vocabulary and sentence structure. The last named category is a far cry from the Bereiter and Engelman programme which seems to suggest that the children have no linguistic resources to draw on and have to learn acceptable vocabulary and structures as though they were learning English as a new language. The programmes which specify vocabulary and structures to be used by the children all seem to be based on the assumption that Standard English is the language of education and that young children must learn to use it. Apart from the Bereiter and Engelman programme, the best known American programme in this country is the Peabody Language Development Kit. This is, in fact, an eclectic type of programme embodying goals from all the above categories except perhaps the last (social interaction).

What then accounts for the good results obtained from experimental situations in which structured programmes are used compared with the poorer results from enrichment programmes, and what do the good results really consist of? Undoubtedly a major factor contributing to good results is that the setting in which children are tested is more similar to the setting in which they have been taught, than it is for children who have experienced the freer kind of pre-school environment. Children who have worked through a programme, however unstructured, have learnt to respond to adults in certain kinds of situations, situations which are often replicated in the testing. They have therefore learnt to display their learning in a way that counts. It is also been suggested that the more structured programmes provide a greater variety of conversational settings than might normally have occurred in the freer type of nursery of pre-school. This may mean that all children can initially feel at home. A programme which gives them access to a stationary adult, and which provides a context in which they can find more security than they do for the rest of the day, is particularly good for children who need attention. Many children have difficulty in attracting it in the hubbub of the traditional nursery school. The times in the day when a programme is followed may give considerable help to children who otherwise tend to prefer non-verbal strategies. Again, the continuity and consistency of the adult-child relationship may be greater in the context of following a programme than otherwise, and this consistency especially may be as important for the child's language development as for his affective development during the pre-school years. The very orderliness and predictability of situations that are structured for a certain part of the day may be an important factor in nursery schools where the noise and spontaneity of activities does not make for audible and sustained conversations.

The measured gains made by children in pre-school intervention programmes show a consistency both in the large-scale American studies and in the much smaller number of studies carried out in Britain. In most cases there often seem to be startling gains very early in the administration of the programme. Secondly, there are gains in IQ as long as the programme lasts, but these tend to tail off when it goes on beyond a year. More importantly, especially for those concerned with decisions about policy and funding, the effects of such programmes tend to 'wash out' after the programme has ended. Although there are exceptions to this pattern, it is borne out by the increasing bulk of evaluation studies (e.g. of the American Head Start programme) and of studies that follow-up the children involved over lengthy periods of up to 5 years. Most of the programmes were in fact for children aged 3 upwards, and it was thought that intervention before the age of three might have better results. But here, too, in at least one project with two-year-olds, the results are disappointing. Children who have followed intervention programmes before the age of three did no better than those who came in later. There is of course the possibility that with children from the most disadvantaged groups in society, the pressure of environmental factors is such that is negates the effects of the children's participation in a pre-school programme of any type.

In linked Head Start — Follow-Through programmes in America, where family services, health and nutritional care have been linked with children's participation in pre-school programmes, it looks as though long-term results may be better. However, the overall evaluation of the American work has led to the depressing conclusion of the Jencks study, *Inequality*, that educational intervention can in fact do little on its own to counteract the disadvantages of the disadvantaged.

The generality of programmes used in America involve small-group teaching, usually for short periods in the day. Within the group, the teacher may focus on individual children for brief interchanges, but the setting is one in which six or more children are involved. An exception to this, and one that has influenced an important development in Britain, is the individual tutorial programme developed by Marion Blank and Francis Solomon in New York in the late 1960s. The basis of this programme is a daily session of 15 to 20 minutes in which individual children work with a teacher separated from the group. The authors question whether early language skills can be fostered in a group situation. They diagnose the main factor in disadvantaged children's lives as a lack of 'an on-going elaborated dialogue' with an adult, and feel therefore that what is needed above all is a one-to-one situation, but one in which the adult plays a deliberate fostering role, teaching the child, through dialogue, to question, probe and investigate.

This combines the advantages of both the structured and child-centred approaches, and above all means that the dialogue can be geared to the child's level. This enables the child to understand what is being taught, or, if he fails, the teacher learns something about the child's failure to understand and therefore comes closer to his real learning problem. Marion Blank felt that in normal nursery situations many of the exchanges between child and teacher pass by without the child necessarily understanding the content of what is said. (The variations in individual development and especially in comprehension mentioned earlier in this paper highlight the probability of this.) Teachers very often provide answers to their own questions, and do not wait for the child to provide one himself, or they assume his ignorance.

The findings of Blank and Solomon influenced some of the decisions made in the British Educational Priority Areas study. The Plowden Report (1967) had advocated a policy of positive discrimination 'to make schools in the most deprived areas as good as the best in the country' and a programme of action research was set up in five local education authorities shortly after the publication of the report to explore ways of operating the Plowden philisophy. In all five areas action and research extended into pre-school education, and included setting up new or traditional forms of educational provision for the under-fives and specific attempts to promote language development of children in the study. Of these, probably the most convincing is the experiment in the West Riding which built on the one-to-one philosophy of the Blank and Solomon programme, though this was in the context of many other group activities in which adults, including parents, helped to stimulate language and develop children's concentration.

In the circumstances in which this experimental work was carried out (including the atmosphere of enthusiasm and excitement that characterized most of the work in the EPA study), it is impossible to evaluate the effect of the programme above. Certainly in this scheme as in others in the EPA study the results show a consistent pattern of children making gains in language skills over the year, and where there was follow-up over a further year, a continuation of progress into the infant school instead of the falling-back that has been recorded in many of the American studies.

The EPA programme also involved the use of the Peabody Language Development Kit, as did an experiment carried out by the National Foundation for Educational Research in five Slough nursery schools. As suggested above, the Peabody Language Kit embodies what we might call an eclectic approach to language development; it is a programme in the sense that it sets out a sequence of 'lessons', each with specific objectives, gives details of methods to be used, and provides materials. It is considerably less formal than the Bereiter and Engelman programme, though many people lump the two together. It emphasizes language for problem solving and reasoning, and general vocabulary development. It includes stories, songs, games and rhymes, as well as models for question-and-answer work. As might be expected, the British tradition of pre-school work makes this kind of scheme unacceptable to many teachers, even if it is a far cry from the most formal of programmes; within the EPA study account is taken of teachers' attitudes to the scheme, and the material was used with some considerable freedom and inventiveness. There was a broad difference of opinion between those who disliked the idea of a specific daily language session (apparently on the grounds that the nursery catered well enough for children's language needs within its normal mode of operation), and those who saw an advantage in setting aside a small part of the day to concentrate on language and welcomed the element of systematicity that this introduced into their work. The results of the testing of children in the EPA scheme are difficult to interpret in a rigorous sense. In the short term, it looks as if the children's language improved and as if the use of the Peabody Language Development Kit itself made a specific contribution to this improvement. While the programme itself has failings that earn it disapproval from British teachers, the EPA results can be taken to imply that it would be worthwhile to develop programmes suited to British nursery schools. A report on the NFER/Slough study is now available (NFER, 1976) but the results seem to fall very much into line with those of the EPA study. Children in the experiment made significant gains in measured language development compared with children in control groups, though in some aspects of language these gains seem to be as great in only two terms of work as in four or more terms. However, two years later there were no significant differences between the school attainment of children who had taken part in the programme and those in the control groups.

It is worth concluding with the observation that in general it seems that disadvantaged children who do not receive any pre-school education (day, nursery, nursery school or play group) tend to fall behind their peers in language development as they grow older. American findings show this very clearly, and small studies carried out within the EPA project provide some evidence, slight though it is, that this is the case in Britain too. However, research findings in America also show that children who have not attended pre-school tend to make a spurt in their reception year at school and that the gains made by children in pre-school programmes tend to disappear once these same children have started school. The follow-up study of British children in the EPA study shows a different trend: the children continued to make progress in the infant school, both in a school where there was a continuation of special provision and in one without. There are many ways of looking at these results, and indeed of explaining them away, though teachers' own assessments of the children seem to support the notion that the pre-school language programmes had been beneficial and contributed to the children's progress in infant schools.

It is clearly dangerous to generalize from the American experience, vast and varied as it seems to be; it may be just as dangerous to generalize from the highly localized experimental situations of the British pre-school language experiments. But they certainly suggest optimism rather than doubt, and point to the need for much more work to be done in preparing and evaluating language programmes in pre-school education in Britain.

Intervention in the home

The bulk of research and experimentation in the use of language programmes in nursery schools or kindergartens is American. However, when we turn to the notion of intervention in the home, and to ways in which this may influence the child's learning of language, there is rather more to learn from English experiments. There is perhaps a welcome realism here in that intervention in the child's education at home recognizes the fact that its importance outweighs the education provided at nursery and infant school. It is clear that in his earliest years the child is learning how to learn, and how to use language for learning. Within the home he relates to parents, other adults, and often to brothers and sisters. He establishes attitudes in respect of other adults and children, and modes of behaviour which will relate to his subsequent behaviour at school. Most importantly, when he is in the early stages of acquiring language, he is with his mother who knows where he is in his progress and can respond — far better than any nursery teacher or other helper — to his early utterances. She understands the idiosyncrasies of his pronunciation and lexicon.

> *'When a child not yet three told his father, "Betty and I played radio last night", his father understood that Betty Bryant, a graduate student, had been there with her tape recorder; but only the child's mother knew that Betty had come earlier that day rather than the previous night, and so only she could correct the child's encoding of past time. Someone outside the family could have said little more than, "Oh, that's nice", while wondering what had been going on.'*

It has been suggested that consistency in adult—child relationships may be as important for language as for affective development during the child's early years.

There are then many reasons that suggest it may be better to influence the way in which mothers talk to and interact with their children in the home, rather than to provide additional facilities in the nursery school. Although there are ethical objections to this suggestion, it has led to several experimental schemes in this country and in America. The best known in Britain is probably the home-visiting scheme carried out in the West Riding within the Educational Priority Area action-research programme. Mothers with a child over the age of 18 months were visited every week and involved in play and activity with the child. The play had a purpose which was explained to the mother, so that in most cases she as well as the child was learning. One of the home visitors' observations was that many mothers assumed that their children would learn basic concepts (e.g. about colour, location) naturally and without help or that they would be learnt at school. These mothers learnt how much more active they themselves could be in promoting their children's learning. It was also found that the children tended to do more when the mothers — not just the home visitor — were working with them. This was not specifically a language programme as such, but the children's language progress was an obvious concomitant of their progress in general. The results recorded in later volumes of the EPA report give very positive support to this kind of scheme as an approach to improving children's language skills.

There is rather more specific information about language in the home, and of techniques used in a home-intervention programme, in an ongoing study at Sheffield conducted by Douglas Hubbard. Again, the parents' views of their own role in their children's development seem important. On the whole they do not see it as an educational role. School will 'bring out' whatever is there in the child's mental endowment. The scheme is thus basically an attempt to influence working class attitudes to parenthood. It is partly directed at preparation for parenthood in school, but partly at influencing parents themselves, mainly through discussions and classes at the welfare clinic. A Norwich scheme comes closer to the EPA model described above, and involves an educational visitor working with the mother, supporting her, and alerting her to aspects of her child's needs which she has not previously considered. Stress is laid on the professional status and skills of the visitor. In a pilot stage of the experiment, a substantial change in family attitudes to their role in the child's linguistic and general development is reported.

These and other parent education schemes in England have had no large-scale evaluation element built in, though all claim successes in attaining their objectives, i.e. change in parents' attitudes to child rearing and school, change in parents' behaviour, and improvement in children's achievement. We do not know whether the changes in parents' attitudes and behaviour are sustained after the programme of visits is finished. American studies present hard evidence on the long-term benefit of parental involvement and show that the children's improvement is sustained even up to three or four years after the visiting stops. Thus in the overall evaluation of American work home visiting comes out a great deal better than the use of special programmes in nursery schools. This is attributed to the fact that home visiting programmes have tended to begin working with children at an early age (e.g. 18 months), and of course that they emphasize one-to-one interaction between a child and an adult, predominantly the mother. Presumably too they make for more sustained and consistent teaching behaviour in between visits than may be possible in the nursery situation where several adults may have to work with comparatively large numbers of children. From all that we have seen of research and observation of infants' language development, the crucial role of the adult, particularly the mother in a one-to-one relationship, makes these results a matter of common sense. Incidentally, evaluation of American studies also suggests that parent education through classes or group discussions is not nearly as effective as education in the home.

Chapter Four

Language Policy in Early Education

All children who are not handicapped in some way learn to talk. The child's acquisition of language has been called one of the most impressive pieces of learning that an individual accomplishes in his life, and, indeed, the more one examines this piece of learning the more impressive it appears. The basic essentials are acquired very rapidly, between one and a half and four years of age. The learner apparently exerts very little effort. He seems to take great pleasure in the process. The adults around him, who might be considered his teachers, apparently do little that is deliberately intended to teach language.

It is clear, however, that the mother's role is crucial in the child's acquisition of language; at the same time there is uncertainty about specific features of her role. Stress is laid on her responsiveness to the very young baby, and later, on her responsiveness to the meanings the child wishes to convey in his earliest utterances. The language she uses in her responses to the child is important in itself; intuitively she modifies her own speech when talking to him. Within this pattern of behaviour, the exact role of imitation, of the grammar of the mother's sentences, and of her development of the child's meanings, is undefined. It may be that there are critical periods in the child's language development when the mother's response is more important than it is at other times. It is impossible to discover how selective young children are in what they take from their linguistic environment. (It seems likely that the ongoing work of Gordon Wells at Bristol University, which involves the recording of children in their homes over a long period, will produce data that go some way to answering these questions.)

In Dr Tough's recent work the concept of the 'fostering' of language, both in the home and in pre-school education, has been more clearly defined than in earlier studies. Her analysis of the different purposes language serves for the three-year-old upwards helps to provide a framework for looking at the fostering qualities of mothers' (and teachers') language. What seems to be needed now are detailed observational studies of mother–child interaction (like those that form the basis of the analysis of children's developing grammars) which can be analysed in Dr Tough's terms. There are enormous practical problems in this, because there is something completely unpredictable about the moments at which the mother's response becomes a 'fostering' response. As suggested by Burton White,

> '*Our most effective mothers do not devote the bulk of their day to rearing their children ... What they seem to do,* often without knowing exactly why, is *to perform excellently the functions of designer and consultant ...*

> *These mothers very rarely spent 5, 10 or 20 minutes teaching their one- or two-year-olds, but they get an enormous amount of teaching in 'on the fly', and usually at the child's instigation. Though they do volunteer comments opportunistically, they mostly act in response to overtures by the child'* (White, 1971).

It is difficult for any research study to catch teaching 'on the fly'; even the most elaborate television recording equipment could hardly cope with the situation of the average infant in the average home. And yet the essence of language fostering lies in this aspect of the mother's interaction with her child.

Earlier sections of this report commented on the preoccupation of researchers with the grammatical features of child language. In recent years the swing away from this to focusing on the child's meaning, and thus on the whole nature of his interaction with his mother and others, brings us to look more closely at the question of what the child can actually do with his language, what functions it serves in his life. This links with the question of linguistic advantage and disadvantage, and thus with the issue of intervention, whether measures can be taken to deliberately foster the language of children whose home environments are such that they do not apparently favour language acquisition. It seems fitting in concluding this report to devote some pages to this question as the report of the Bullock Committee, *A Language for Life*, has restated the case for intervention and in so doing has possibly drawn a blueprint for a language policy in early education in this country.

To intervene or not to intervene

When the report of the Plowden Committee (1967) on primary education made its case for *positive discrimination*, i.e. for taking special steps to improve the quality of education provided in schools, largely in the inner city areas of priority need, there were few objections of a genuine political kind. The late 1960s and early 1970s, however, have seen the stirrings of a radical political awareness that has made the discussion more elaborate and, one hopes, more sensitive.

Many voices, not all of them those of researchers, have questioned the work of Bernstein and other sociological-educationists, and, as suggested earlier, attacked some of the implications it seems to have had for educational policy. The suggestion is that in adopting a superficial assessment of children's language skills, one is dismissing or ignoring the language they have in order to try to replace it with one that it seems socially desirable for them to have. Indeed, the social and educational aspects of this argument are closely interwoven, for the form of language that the researchers (and teachers) are accused of ignoring or dismissing is often a non-standard dialect (e.g. forms of Black English in America, or of Caribbean dialects in Britain), alien to the teacher and not valued by the majority. The work of Labov and other American linguists is used to support this argument, especially their studies of 'non-verbal' children and adolescents in situations where they are in fact verbal, i.e. where they are not put at a social disadvantage or expected to talk in a way that may be alien to them, e.g. in a dialect which is totally different from the dialect of the home, or which is associated with hostile authority figures. Labov suggests that 'lower class' language need be no less effective or less valid than, for instance, standard English when it is used with acceptable and complex grammatical forms. The arguments sustained by Labov and others have perhaps been put strongly as a corrective to the view that children's home language is worthless and that some children bring, as it were, nothing of their own to school — a view, incidentally, upheld by the Newbolt Report on English only 50 years ago:

> *'Teachers of English sometimes complain that when the children come to school they can scarcely speak a word at all. They should regard this as an advantage'* (HMSO, 1921).

The teacher who wishes to start 'where the child is', to do justice to his language and, for instance, to recognize his dialect as valid, *is* in a dilemma. Labov's argument, taken to its logical conclusion, could prevent one embarking on any form of language intervention. But it is worth pointing out that Labov's work does not as yet offer insights into the different abilities of individual lower class speakers to deal with different situations. It does not explore the functional aspects of language in early education or answer the fundamental question posed by Dr Tough's work. Some children come to nursery school already skilled in using language for purposes that will ultimately make for a measure of success in formal education, while others at that age use language for a more restricted range of purposes. Can the nursery teacher in her interaction with children help those in the latter category to widen their range of language functions?

In this country other arguments have been advanced for not intervening in the child's language learning in the nursery (and infant) school. These were glanced at in the preceding chapter and are based on the fear that if special attention is paid to language, then it will create an imbalance in the pre-school curriculum. The social and emotional aspects of the child's education will be at risk, and a formal aspect introduced into an environment that should be kept totally free and informal. No doubt it was fears of this kind that partly accounted for some teachers' negative reactions to the Peabody Language Development Kit. The same fears originally impeded the introduction into British nursery and infant schools of special language work for those minority-group children who could speak little or no English. A more realistic sense of priorities in the mid-seventies, for these children's language needs as for those of others, means that teachers may be at least more open to suggestions for specific language work with young children. It is in this climate of opinion that the Bullock Report puts the case:

'All children should be helped to acquire as wide a range as possible of the uses of language and there are clearly two ways in which this can be achieved. The first consists in helping parents to understand the process of language development in their children and to take part in it. The second resides in the skill and knowledge of the nursery and infant teacher, her measured attention to the child's precise language needs, and her inventiveness in creating situations which bring about their fulfilment' (5.10).

While not dismissing the work of Labov and others, the report clearly makes the case for all children to develop the use of the kind of language that is important for learning in the school situation. It makes a distinction between the fact that all children apparently have the ability to use complex language (*vide* Bernstein, page 27), but that some do not habitually encounter situations in which they have to use that ability:

'If a child does not encounter situations in which he has to explore, recall, predict, plan, explain, and analyse, he cannot be expected to bring to school a ready made facility for such uses. What is needed is to create the contexts and conditions in which this ability can develop' (5.9).

Research needs
If the money is available, *it seems clear that the Bullock Report will boost experimentation in both parent education and pre-school language intervention. The work carried out under the Head Start Programme in

---

*The present clampdown on educational spending was not envisaged when this report was written.

America and the Educational Priority Areas scheme in Britain, described in the previous chapter, has contributed greatly to our knowledge in these two areas. The curriculum development project on Communication Skills in Early Childhood, based on Dr Tough's research and directed by her, will probably remain for many years the largest single effort in this country to guide teachers in both the appraisal and fostering of young children's early language skills.

The pattern of events over the last 15 years suggests that a crucial area for research is now not simply language intervention itself — in the home or in the nursery — but the effectiveness of different approaches to educating the educators (and utlimately the policy makers). Where should language education begin? Should we be thinking of *education and language,* as in the Bullock Report's suggestions for including it in child development courses for fourth and fifth year secondary school pupils, in talks for mothers at welfare clinics, and in social-education programmes — possibly disguised as fiction — on television? If some nursery and infant teachers are resistant to the idea of introducing specific language work, how important is it that they should gain deeper insights into language through in-service courses? What form should the language component take, recommended for *all* students in initial training by the Bullock Committee?

The growth in academic courses of study in linguistics in Britain has no doubt contributed to the interest in child language acquisition and in the role of language in education, two issues which have come to assume central importance in educational theory in the 1970s. It would, however, be a mistake to think that these same academic courses held the key to the problems of teacher and parent education. In recommending that

> '*All teachers in training, irrespective of the age-range they intend to teach, should complete satisfactorily a substantial course in language and reading*' (rec. 308).

the Bullock Report stressed the need for theory to be linked to practice, and by implication deplored the tendency for the academic element in students' training to be developed at the expense of the professional element. In pleading for the role of language in the classroom to form a substantial part of language courses for teachers, it suggests that there is a middle ground, between linguistic theory and actual teaching, where the need for teachers' understanding and insight is greatest. The examples of language courses given in the Report (to form a basis for work on language in initial training, and to lead to continuing work in in-service courses) lay emphasis on developmental aspects of language from the infant's acquisition of it upwards, on the differences between forms, e.g. between dialects, between speech and writing, and on the functions of language in different contexts, including the classroom.

A teacher's awareness of children's language development relates not only to what he (or she) understands *about* language, but also to his being able to appraise or assess children's language. This is true too for the parents. If they are to monitor their child's progress in any way, and to modify their behaviour to help the child improve his performance, then they must be able to make informed judgments about the child. In so doing they will be scrutinizing their own behaviour and the way they interact with the child. To develop skills of appraisal in teachers who have a professional interest in developing them, and in parents who do not have the same motive, is a demanding task. Considerably more experimentation is called for than we have at present available to us (in Dr Tough's work, and in the EPA experiment), and the role of closed-circuit television, as of public television, as an instrument of training may be particularly important.

All the recommendations for improvements in nursery school provision, for the deployment of extra adults in nursery (and infant schools), for home visiting and for parent education, relate to vital questions of training. Recent research reviews, like that of Barbara Tizard, show a considerable amount of research to be going on, some of which may indeed provide more specific answers to questions raised here about language development. But if we are concerned with intervention, then we need answers to equally important questions about deployment and training staff, otherwise little visible success may come out of apparently improved situations. A review and comparison of types of language training for staff at different levels would provide a base-line for the definition of further action, as would an overview of current initiatives in parent education. The long-term monitoring and evaluation of different types of training provision is also called for. However, it is true to say with the Bullock Report that although there is much that remains to be learned, *there is much that has been learned that remains to be used.* One suspects that in the field of teacher education this is particularly apt, and that already, in the area of language education, a vast resource of useful experience is waiting to be tapped if only a useful means can be found of bringing the information together and analysing it.

Chapter Five

An Introductory Reading List

The basic reading on child language acquisition ranges from the pleasingly familiar and readily accessible discussions of children talking to the taxing and recondite exploration of linguistic theory at all its levels. Teachers, parents or educationists who wish to inform themselves more fully about how children acquire language, really need to explore the literature in all directions. There is as much danger in failing to come to grips with some of the theoretical issues as there is in concentrating solely on theory at the expense of what is both practical and practicable. The intention therefore in providing this short annotated booklist is to help the initiate in the field to make a few key choices about where he puts both his time and his money.

Louis BLOOM (1970): *Language Development: Form and Function in Emerging Grammars.* MIT Press.

This book is based on a longwinded study of three children, Kathryn, Gia and Eric. Their spontaneous speech was recorded and transcribed, and grammatical analyses were made, which showed the 'different' grammars each child had acquired at various points in time (between the ages of 1.0 and 2.0, two of Kathryn's grammars, three of Eric's, and two of Gia's). Bloom's transcriptions included notes on the 'non-linguistic' setting, so that sense could be made of even the most telegraphic of the children's utterances. Bloom tried to show that the child does in fact intend to express meanings something like those adults attribute to him when they expand his utterances, and also can intend different meanings when using the same utterance on different occasions, e.g. *Mommy sock* (= 'That's mummy's sock', and 'Mummy is putting on my sock'). Bloom thus draws the distinction between the *surface structure* of child's speech, and the more complex *deep structure,* or *meaning,* which is part of the same child's competence.

James BRITTON (1970): *Language and Learning.* Allan Lane.

A book that draws on philosophy, linguistics, psychology and child development — and also on the author's experience as parent and teacher. It traces the development of speech and writing, linked throughout to the theory that we use language as a means of organizing a representation of the world: 'the representation so created constitutes the world we operate in, the basis of all the predictions by which we set the course of our lives.' Language both in the home and school is discussed, and the development of the cognitive processes. Perhaps because of its copious use of transcripts of children's talk, perhaps too because of the author's lucid style, it has a deceptive simplicity and readibility. It reads as a non-technical treatise, but in fact makes great — and satisfying — demands on the reader.

Roger Brown (1973): *A First Language — the Early Stages.* George Allen & Unwin.

This book presents the findings of the longitudinal study of language acquisition conducted by Brown and his colleagues at Harvard (and heralded at an earlier stage in the work by the Bellugi and Brown Paper(s) listed in the references). Three children's developing language was recorded, and both the grammatical and semantic aspects of their speech analysed. In passing, the study reviews and draws on the existing literature, and traces the development of various theories, including that of 'pivot' grammar (which it discounts).

Brown established 5 stages of linguistic development, related not to the children's chronological age but the length of their utterances. Stage I takes the child to the threshold of the development of syntax, when words are combined to make sentences. Brown demonstrates how those sentences are always limited to the same small set of meanings (nomination, recurrence ('Again'), disappearance, attribution, possession, agency, and a few others). In Stage II modulations occur to basic structural meanings, so that the child begins to express number, time and aspect. In other words, he begins to use inflections and case-makers, prepositions and articles. The order in which these 'modulations' are acquired is almost identical across children, the relatively simpler grammatical and semantic features being acquired first.

Courtney CAZDEN (1972): *Child Language and Education.* Holt, Rinehart and Winston.

The author writes: 'One purpose of this book is to help its readers listen more reflectively to children by describing some of the ways in which behavioural scientists are studying child language, and by giving some examples of what they are finding out.' The readers are described as any who are interested in seeking to improve children's communicative adequacy through education. Modern linguistic theory is explained lucidly and the link with practical concerns maintained throughout. Discussions of educational implications are down-to-earth, enlightened with reference to actual situations and to classroom practitioners.

M.M. LEWIS (1963): *Language, Thought and Personality in Infancy and Childhood.* Harrap.

This is a systematic account of the growth of the child's language in relation to his general development in infancy and childhood. For this reason, and perhaps too because it lacks the close analytical linguists' approach of most of the other works cited in this paper, it is a more readable and more human document than the others. It is certainly the best introduction to child language acquisition for the non-linguist, and invaluable for its introduction to the relation of language to thought, and to the child's social and ethical development.

Paula MENYUK (1971): *The Acquisition and Development of Language.* Prentice-Hall.

Paula Menyuk's book offers a very readable discussion of the basic issues in language acquisition, including the physiological readiness of the child to acquire language and the processes involved. The development of phonology (the systematic basis of pronunciation), syntax and semantics is discussed, and in particular the sequence in which the child undertstands and produces the structures. The child's acquisition of the linguistic system is related to his physiological and intellectual development, and there is an interesting account of deviant language behaviour. It makes for a fairly stiff read, and deals with research evidence in depth, but in such a way that its relevance is always clear. This might be the best in-depth study from a linguistic angle for the non-linguist to graduate to after Cazden.

Joan TOUGH (1974): *Focus on Meaning.* Allen and Unwin.

An eminently readable book which includes an account of the early stages of children's language development and of the parents' role in promoting it. Many transcripts of recorded conversations are given and analysed in a practical straightforward way, to show the range of uses for which language can serve the child. The nursery and infant teacher's role is also discussed, and, as the title indicates, the focus throughout is on the meaning of the child's (and adults') language. 'The focus on meaning necessitates insight not only into the child's and the teacher's talk but embraces the purpose of all our activities in school'.

Frederick WILLIAMS (ed) (1970): *Language and Poverty — Perspectives on a Theme.* Markham Pub. Co.

This volume provides a useful overview of the social context in which acquisition and development of language has become a key consideration in the last ten years. It incorporates papers by linguists, psychologists and sociologists, which look at the problems of urban (and rural) education in multi-ethnic America. These include the specific problems of bilingual and non-standard dialect speakers, and of the deaf, and of assessing the language of disadvantaged children. Intervention in preschool education and its sociological and philosophical implications are also discussed from different points of view, e.g. 'The kinds of changes proposed may help to overcome some of the language disabilities stemming from a language-poor home environment. They will, however, be seen by the child and his parents as irrelevant if the child's schooling appears to lead nowhere except onto the front stoop and into the street. If the disadvantaged child and his parents do not see schooling as a means of achieving equal opportunity, if the society is not able to demonstrate the relevance of education, its relation to a man's life chances, then no educational changes are sufficient to alter the charge that education is irrelevant to the lives of disadvantaged children.'

BIBLIOGRAPHY and REFERENCES

BERSTEIN, B. (1961) 'Social class and linguistic development: a theory of social learning.' In A.H. HALSEY, FLOUD, and C.A. ANDERSON (eds.), *Education, Economy and Society.* Glencoe, III: Free Press.

BERNSTEIN, B. and HENDERSON, D. 'Social class differences in the relevance of language to socialization,' *Sociology,* in press.

BLOOM, L.M. (1970) *Language Development: form and function in emerging grammars.* Cambridge, Mass.: MIT Press.

BRITTON, J. (1970) *Language and Learning.* Allen Lane.

BRONFENBRENNER, U. (1973) *Is Early Intervention Effective?* Washington: Department of Health, Education and Welfare.

BROWN, R. (1968) 'The development of wh-questions in child speech,' *Journal of Verbal Learning and Verbal Behaviour.*

BROWN, R. (1973) *A First Language.* Cambridge, Mass.: Harvard University Press. First published in Great Britain by George Allen & Unwin Ltd.

BROWN, R. and BELLUGI, U. (1964) 'Three processes in the child's acquisition of syntax,' *Harvard Educational Review.*

BROWN, R. and FRASER' C. (1964) 'The acquisition of syntax.' In: BELLUGI, U. and BROWN, R. (eds.) *The Acquisition of Language. Monographs of the Society for Research in Child Development.*

BRUNER, S. (1975) 'poverty and childhood,' *Oxford Review of Education,* 1, 1.

CASHDAN, A. and GRUGEON, Elizabeth (1972) *Language in Education.* Open University set book. Routledge & Kegan Paul in association with the Open University Press.

CAZDEN, C.B. (1965) Environmental assistance to the child's acquisition of grammar. Unpublished doctoral dissertation, Harvard University.

CAZDEN, C.B. (1967) 'The role of parent speech in the acquisition of grammar,' *Project Literacy Reports.* No. 8. Ithaca, NY: Cornell University.

CAZDEN, C.B. (1970) 'The neglected situation in child language research and education.' In: Frederick WILLIAMS (ed.) *Language and Poverty: perspectives on theme.* Chicago: Markham. Expanded version in *Journal of Social Issues.*

CAZDEN, C.B. (1971) 'Evaluating Language learning in early childhood education.' In: BLOOM, B.S., HASTING, T. and MADAUS, G. (eds.) *Handbook on Formative and Summative Evaluation of Student Learning.* McGraw-Hill.

CAZDEN, C.B. (1972) *Language in Early Childhood Education.* Washington, D.C.: National Association for the Education of Young Children.

CAZDEN, C.B. (1975) Concentrated and Contrived Encounters:

suggestions for language assessment in early childhood education. Unpublished paper, delivered to SSRC Conference in Language and Learning, Leeds.

CAZDEN, C.B., JOHN, Vera P., and HYMES, D. (1972) *Functions of Language in the Classroom.* New York: Teachers College Press, Columbia University.

CENTRAL ADVISORY COUNCIL FOR EDUCATION (ENGLAND) (1967) *Children and their Schools* (The Plowden Report). London: HMSO.

CHOMSKY, C.S. (1969) *The Acquisition of Syntax in Children from 5 to 10.* Cambridge, Mass.: MIT Press.

CHOMSKY, N. (1965) *Aspects of the Theory of Syntax.* MIT Press.

CILT (1974) Reports and Papers 10. *The space between ...* Papers from a conference on language in the middle years of secondary education held at the Manchester Teachers' Centre, 20—22 November 1973. Centre for Information on Language Teaching and Research.

COLEMAN, J.S. (1966) *Equality of Educational Opportunity.* Washington, DC: US Department of Health, Education and Welfare, Office of Education.

DAVIS, A. (1975) *Problems of Language and Learning.* Heinemann in association with the SSRC and SSRE.

ERVINN-TRIPP, S. (1971) 'Social background and verbal skills.' In: HUXLEY, R. and INGRAM, E. (eds.) *Language Development: models and methods.* New York: Academic Press.

FERGUSON, A. and SLOBIN, D. (1973) *Studies of Child Language Development.* Holt, Rinehart and Winston, Inc.

FLAVELL, J.H. *et al.* 1968) *The Development of Role-Taking and Communications Skills in Children.* New York: Wiley.

GAHAGAN, D.M. and GAHAGAN, G.A. (1970) *Talk Reform: explorations in language in primary school.* Primary socialization, language and education, Vol. III. Sociological Research Unit Monograph Series directed by B. Bernstein. Beverly Hills, California: Sage Publications.

HALSEY, A.H. (1972) *Education Priority,* Volume I. EPA Problems and Policies. Report of a research project sponsored by the Department of Education and Science and the Social Science Research Council. HMSO.

HATCH, E. (1969) *The Syntax of Four Reading Programs Compared with Language Development of Children.* Inglewood, Calif.: Southwestern Regional Laboratory for Educational Research and Development. TR 21, 22.

HESS, R.D. and SHIPMAN, V. (1968) 'Maternal influences upon early learning.' In: HESS, R.D. and BEAR, R.M. (eds.) *Early Education.* Chicago: Aldine.

HMSO (1921) *The Teaching of English in England.*

HYMES, D. (1971) 'Competence and performance in linguistic theory.' In: HUXLEY, R. and INGRAM, E. (eds.) *Language Acquisition: models and methods.* New York: Academic Press.

JENCKS, C., *et al.* (1972) *Inequality. A reassessment of the effect of family and schooling in America.* Basic Books, Inc. U.S.

LABOV, W. (1969) 'The logic of non-standard English,' *The Florida F.L. Reporter.*

LAVATELLI, C.S. (1969) *Language Training in Early Childhood Education.* University of Illinois Press.

LAWTON, D. (1968) *Social Class, Language and Education.* London: Routledge & Kegan Paul.

LENNEBERG, E.H. (1967) *Biological Foundation of Language.* New York: Wiley.

LEWIS, M.M. (1963) *Language, Thought and Personality in Infancy and Childhood.* George G. Harrap & Co. Ltd.

LUNT, Helen N. (1973) *Language and Language Teaching — current research in Britain 1971–1972.* Centre for Information on Language Teaching and Research: Longman.

LURIA, A.R. and YUDOVICH, F. la. (1971) *Speed and the Development of Mental Processes in the Child.* Harmondsworth: Penguin Books.

MENYUK, P. (1969) *Sentences Children Use.* Cambridge, Mass.: MIT Press.

MOORE, T.E. (1973) *Cognitive Development and the Acquisition of Language.* New York and London: Academic Press.

NATIONAL FOUNDATION FOR EDUCATIONAL RESEARCH IN ENGLAND AND WALES (1976). *An Experiment in Nursery Education.* Slough: NFER.

NELSON, Katherine (1973) *Structure and Strategy in Learning to Talk. Monographs of the Society for Research in Child Development* Vol. 38, Nos. 1–2. University of Chicago Press.

SHIELDS, M.M. (1972) *Report on an Investigation of the Development of Language Skill in Children between Three and Five Years.* SSRC.

SMITH, F. and MILLER, G.A. (eds.) (1966) *The Genesis of Language.* MIT Press.

SMITH, G. (1975) *Educational Priority,* Volume 4: The West Riding Project. Report of a research project sponsored by the Department of Education and Science and the Social Science Research Council. H.M.S.O.

TEMPLIN, M.C. (1957) *Certain Langauge Skills in Children: their development and inter-relationships.* University of Minnesota Press.

TIZARD, Barbara (1974) *Pre-School Education in Great Britain — a research review.* SSRC.

TIZARD, B., COOPERMAN, O., JOSEPH, A. and TIZARD, O. 'Environmental effects on language development: a study of young children in long-stay residential nurseries,' *Child Development,* in press.

TOUGH, Joan (1973) *Focus on Meaning — Talking to some Purpose with Young Children.* George Allen & Unwin Ltd.

TOUGH, Joan (1974) *Listening to Children Talking.* A draft guide to language appraisal. (To be published for the Schools Council).

VYGOTSKY, L.S. (1962) *Thought and Language.* Cambridge, Mass.: MIT Press.

WEIR, Ruth (1962) *Language in the Crib.* The Hague: Mouton.

WHITE, B. (1971) 'An analysis of excellent early educational practices: preliminary report,' *Interchange,* Ontario Institute for Studies in Education 2 quoted in CAZDEN (1970)

WIGHT, J. and NORRIS, R.A. (1969) *Teaching of English to West Indian Children.* Report No. 2 University of Birmingham School of Education.

WILLIAMS, F. (ed.) (1970) *Language and Poverty — Perspectives on a Theme.* Chicago: Markham Pub. Co.